Aase Strømstad

The Norwegian Kitchen

Translated by Mary Lee Nielsen

Boksenteret

Contents

© Boksenteret A/S 1999
Layout: Anne Andresen
Coverdesign: Elin Sollesnes, Boksenteret A/S
Repro: Capella Media
Printing and binding: New Interlitho, Italy, 1999

All food photos including title page: Alf Börjesson
Props: Kari Osvold

Coverphoto:
Rolf Sørensen and Ole P. Rørvik/Aune forlag
Other photos:
Torbjørn Moen: Endsheet and pp. 2, 17, 21, 25, 45
Helge Sunde: Verso title page, p. 54
Intra Media/TBP: pp. 4, 30
NPS/Jan-Petter Lahall: p. 18
NN/ Samfoto, Pål Hermansen: p. 40
Øystein Søby/NN/Samfoto: p. 48
Lisa Westgaard: p. 55

ISBN 82-7683-260-1

Props kindly provided by:
Acanthus/Atelier Hødnebø, David Andersen, Bjørn
Seim Antikviteter, Format, Hadeland Glassverk,
Husfliden, Landheim, Magnor Glassverk, Norway
Designs, Norsk Stålpress, Nøstetangen Glass,
Porsgrunds Porselænsfabrik, Sandvika Veveri,
Seiersborg, Turiform.

Enquiries should be sent to the publisher:
Boksenteret forlag
P.O. Box 3125 Elisenberg
0207 Oslo, Norway

Telephone: (47) 22 54 07 00
Fax: (47) 22 54 07 07
E-mail: bsred@boksenteret.no

Foreword

In this little book I have tried to give a glimpse of Norwegian food culture, food habits and eating patterns as they have existed for generations and as they exist to a large extent down to this day. In a country like ours where the climate is not really suited to agriculture and where even the fishing is often restricted by the weather, it is clear that food has always been simply, some would even say crudely, prepared. In many parts of Norway there has been little variation in the diet over the years. Everyday meals were apt to be meager. On the other hand, nothing was spared for holiday feasts or for company. On such occasions tradition still calls for the best that the house can provide.

It has not been easy to single out recipes that are typical of everyday meals, holiday fare and company menus. I have done my best to choose representative dishes from the wide selection of traditional recipes enjoyed in our long, long country. I hope they will give an idea of how well Norwegians eat in the city as well as in the country.

All recipes serve 4 persons, if nothing else is mentioned.

Caser Strömstad

Norwegian food traditions – Norwegian food culture

The need for food is of prime importance no matter where on this earth people live. Not everyone has been able to eat his fill every day. This has also been the case in Norway.

Our varied landscape with its fjords and mountains, forests and heaths, has little arable land. This has influenced food customs and culture throughout the ages. While in some parts of the country people have lived isolated and secluded lives, almost up to modern times, those who lived in coastal areas have looked out on the world and sought contact with other countries and cultures. This has made for regional differences in attitudes and habits. Life styles in the city and the country have also differed widely. In the country people lived as far as possible on the produce of the land, including fish from the fjords and game from the forests and mountains. City dwellers, on the other hand, had early access to imported foods such as rice, spices and raisins. Because of this one finds many old recipes for spice cakes, seasoned sauces and puddings and desserts made with rice and raisins. But the cities were small and widely spaced. Thus, when we speak of traditional Norwegian food and food culture, we think primarily of indigenous, home grown ingredients.

The first people who moved to this northern clime after the ice age were nomads who lived along the coast. The men hunted and fished, and the women prepared the food over an open fire. In time, these wanderers settled down and began to cultivate the soil. Food and cooking methods became more varied. The daily diet was still simple, however. Bread and porridge were made from coarsely ground flour, meat and fish were dried and salted. Fresh foods were reserved for special occasions such as christenings, weddings, funerals and important holidays. First and most important of these occasions was Christmas. Then the porridge was rich and smooth, the flatbread and *lefse* made of finely ground flour and rolled paper thin.

The need to preserve food from season to season has been greater in our country than in many others. Our climate with its short growing season and long, cold, dark winters has resulted in poor harvests. All produce had to be brought into house and barn in the course of a couple of short summer months. Meat producing domestic animals were only butchered in the fall, and when snow, frost and winter storms set in even fishing and hunting were curtailed. Thus it was necessary to dry, smoke and salt meat and fish. Milk was rarely used fresh. It was soured, churned to butter or made into cheese. Grain was mostly of poor quality and did not usually keep for more than a season. Therefore it was baked into unleavened flatbread which would keep for years if stored dry in the storehouse or *stabbur*.

There were also few alternative methods for preparing the food. For a long time the open fireplace served both as heat source and stove. Over the fire an iron kettle was hung on the *skjerdingen*, an iron rod indented at intervals so the kettle could be moved to regulate the heat. Almost everything was boiled in the kettle, porridge, soup, meat and fish. Flatbread and *lefser*

Traditional foods such as fenalår, salted leg of lamb, ham and many kinds of smoked and salted sandwich meats served with potato salad, sour cream and flatbread are excellent summer fare, but taste good at any time of year.

were baked on stone flags, later on sheets of iron, over the coals. Yeast bread as we know it was rare until the 17th century. City bakeries were the first to bake bread in masonry ovens. Only much later do we find ovens in a few kitchens, and not until iron cooking stoves moved into private dwellings was leavened bread commonly baked at home.

With the invention of cast iron molds that could withstand the heat of the coals, came the waffle iron and its many relatives. The molds were cast at home on the farm or in the town smithy. They were richly decorated, often with the initials of the owner and the year in which they were made.

From all of these roots Norwegian food practices and dishes have developed down to our own day.

How we eat today

Never before our own time has such a variety of meat, fish, vegetables, fruits, berries and grains been available in Norway. Today foods of all kinds may be bought year round. The old seasons have been erased for good and bad. Modern methods of preservation, first and foremost freezing, and the import of foodstuffs from every corner of the world have completely changed our eating habits. Furthermore, we travel more and are inspired by other food traditions, tempted by unusual dishes. At the same time we are conscious of our own traditonal food and foodculture. We have also learned that fried foods are unhealthy, so that boiled meat and fish have again become popular. Today we eat cured, salted and smoked foods, *lefser* and flatbread for the sake of variation and because we like the flavor. These are foods we serve our guests with pride.

Norwegian eating patterns

We Norwegians are known as a bunch of eccentrics. This is reflected in our whole way of life, as well as in our eating habits which are different from those of other countries. For one thing, bread is the main ingredient at two meals, in fact, often at three meals, especially for those who are engaged in heavy physical labor.

Breakfast was traditionally a hearty meal with whole wheat bread, butter and various sandwich spreads: sardines, pickled herring, liver paté, cold cuts, cheese and jam. Some preferred oatmeal with sugar and milk. Milk, soured or sweet, coffee or tea were usually drunk at breakfast. For most modern families breakfast is now a simpler meal, perhaps just a bowl of cereal with milk and jam, orange juice and coffee.

At lunch bread is also basic. Many still bring their own open-faced sandwiches to nursery school, school or work. We quip that these lunches always include "one with yellow cheese, one with brown cheese", but both the number of sandwiches and the choice of spread vary widely. Open-faced sandwiches are always in our backpacks on hikes, at the beach or on board our boats, along with a thermos of coffee, cocoa or hot black currant juice. In the backpack we also stow oranges and chocolate to be eaten between meals on long hikes and ski trips.

A good Norwegian breakfast is a nourishing meal that provides energy for the day's many activities. Whole grain breads with different sandwich spreads, eggs – if not every day at least on Saturday and Sunday – milk, juice or fresh fruit, coffee or tea.

Dinner is the most important meal of the day. In the country it is still served at noon, but in the city it is usually eaten around 5 o'clock. A good dinner consists of fish or meat with potatoes, vegetables and, let me not forget, a filling gravy or simple white sauce, depending on the accompaniment. Dessert is rarely a part of everyday dinners now, being reserved for Sundays and parties. Traditionally, however, dessert was served every day. It was a cheap and filling way to save on the more expensive main course. Because of this custom we have many recipes for simple puddings based on grains and flour. Party desserts, on the contrary, have always included lots of cream and eggs with fruit and berries in season.

An early dinner means that we are often hungry at bedtime. In most homes this evening meal consists of several slices of bread with cheese or other spreads, though porridge is sometimes eaten, washed down with a glass of milk, coffee or tea. Nowadays this meal is usually only eaten in families with small children where the day starts early and appetites are large. Most Norwegians, however, eat little or nothing in the evening these days, though many do like a glass of wine and a bit of cheese before bed.

Coffe and cake

Most Norwegians want a piece of cake or a cookie with their after dinner coffee, but on important occasions coffee and cakes constitute a separate and very filling meal. Anywhere from 10 to 15 cakes may grace the table: elegant yeast coffee cakes, layer cakes with lots of whipped cream, two or three loaf cakes and a choice selection of the house's homemade cookies. This elaborate spread may be served late in the evening or right after dinner before drinks.

We are often invited out for just coffee and cakes and are then likely to find the same large array described above. With this in mind, it is not strange to find that most Norwegian housewives are still skillful bakers.

Coffee and cakes can be a meal in themselves. In front Prince cake (recipe p. 53), the macaroon wreath cake tower rises behind (recipe p.53) and a moist cream layer cake with whipped cream and berries is in the middle of the table (recipe p.51).

The open-faced sandwich, a meal in itself

While the daily lunch, whether carried to school or work in a bag or enjoyed at home, is a simple affair, the open-faced sandwiches we serve to guests are elaborate and impressive. Nothing is spared. Shellfish such as shrimp and lobster, fine liver patés, paper thin slices of roast beef and ham, smoked salmon, *gravlaks* and well ripened cheeses. All this is laid out in great quantities on thinly sliced dark or white bread with butter, mayonnaise and other condiments. The garnishes are chosen to accentuate the flavor, consistency and color of the spread, feathery green dill on smoked salmon, a strip of red bell pepper on yellow cheese. A large platter of sandwiches is a feast for the eye as well as the palate.

Open-faced sandwiches, whole or cut in quarters, and canapés that are a mere delicious mouthful are often served at receptions, christenings, important birthdays, funerals and family get-togethers, accompanied by mineral water, soft drinks or wine and rounded off with coffee and a layer cake or a yeast coffee cake.

Christmas traditions

Christmas is the holiday that lays claim to most of our deeply rooted traditions. For Norwegians the real celebration takes place on December 24th. When Christmas is rung in at five o'clock on Christmas Eve, peace descends on mankind and the animal kingdom. A bowl of porridge awaits the Christmas elf in the barn, a sheaf of grain hangs from a branch for the birds, the cattle in their stanchions have an extra bundle of hay, and all the food for the family is stored indoors ready for the long-awaited Christmas holiday. The house has been thoroughly cleaned and decorated, the Christmas tree is in place and hung with all the old, familiar ornaments. The air is heavy with wonderful, mouth-watering odors.

Christmas is the time for family and friends. Then we go from house to house, eating, visiting and enjoying ourselves. In many families special games belong to Christmas, like Old Maid and Go Fish, games that both grown-ups and children can enjoy.

Each part of the country has its own traditional Christmas dinner. In the Eastern provinces and some other parts of Norway, roast loin of pork with crackling, pork patties and small pork sausages, sauerkraut and tiny, meaty potatoes grace the table. In the south, the Christmas cod curls its tail in the pot. It is served with melted butter with or without chopped parsley, and boiled potatoes. In the west and northwest, they swear by *pinnekjøtt*, lamb ribs, dried and salted, then steamed for several hours on barked birch or juniper twigs. *Pinnekjøtt* is served with mashed rutabaga and potatoes. *Lutefisk*, cod soaked in lye, with all the delicious sauces that go with it, is the traditional Christmas dinner for many, while in Trøndelag some still serve both *lutefisk* and roast pork. And in Røros, unlike everywhere else, lightly salted trout and sour cream porridge are Christmas staples – served up together on the same plate. Nowadays, not

Whether young or old, we still prefer to bring a lunch box with open-faced sandwiches to school or to work. A hot or cold beverage is always included.

The cold buffet, traditional at Christmas and at Norwegian hotels and mountain resorts, offers a wide selection of foods: herring, fish, pressed meats, cold roast pork, cheeses – including the typical Norwegian gamalost or "old cheese" and geitost, a sweet brown cheese made from the whey of goat milk – nourishing whole grain breads and butter. Desserts, to be eaten after the cheeses, are also on the table.

*"All seven kinds"
and even more –
our cake tins are
filled to the top with
rich, crisp cookies at
Christmas.*

everyone sticks to such regional traditions. Both ptarmigan and reindeer are popular with many Norwegians, and as country people move to the city, city people to the country, they bring their customs with them.

Desserts on Christmas Eve also vary from place to place, though they are not as bound by tradition as the main course. Rice cream, made from leftover rice pudding from the noonday meal mixed with plenty of whipped cream and flavored with a red berry sauce, is served in many homes. In areas where cloudberries grow they are a popular dessert, sweetened and mixed with whipped cream. A delicious caramel custard made with many eggs and gently steamed in the oven is a treat, as are cream mousses and, of course, ice cream.

And then the cakes appear! Small, rich, crisp cookies made with lots of butter and eggs and shaped on special irons or by hand. At least seven different kinds, as all good housewives know. Berlin wreathes, poor man, hartshorn, pepper cakes, serina cookies, sand nuts, curled wafers, *strull*, *goro*, and many, many more. The first glimpse of the huge platter of Christmas cakes makes everyone's mouth water. Then there are loaf cakes studded with raisins, almonds and dried fruits. Later in the evening nuts, dates, figs, oranges and other fruits arrive on the scene, not to mention marzipan and chocolates.

The cold buffet – confusing and delicious

In many homes it is traditional to offer a cold buffet to guests on Christmas day. The custom undoubtedly stems from the time when it was usual to let the Christmas dinner table remain laid until the next day in case hungry guests should show up late at night. The table is laden to the limit with everything from pickled herring to sweet desserts and can be difficult to approach for anyone who is exposed to the confusion for the first time. Many tourists recall with dismay their initial encounter with the lavish lunch table at their Norwegian hotel. Overwhelmed and untaught, they heap their plate with a hodgepodge of salty and sweet foods. They are apt to be disappointed when nothing tastes good, nor does it look very appetizing all piled willy-nilly together. But when one knows how to attack a buffet of this sort, one realizes that it is both a practical and satisfying way to feed a crowd. Everyone can find something he likes, and everyone can eat as much or as little as he likes without interference from an overly helpful hostess. First of all, it is not only permissible but almost obligatory to help oneself over and over again. Norwegians start with the salty foods such as herring and fish, continue with the meats and cheeses and close with the sweet desserts. Beer and aquavit are usually served with the buffet, but mineral water and cold drinks are always on hand.

Café Life

In the last few decades a myriad of restaurants and cafés have appeared on the scene in Norway. From early morning until late at night one can eat quickly and simply or enjoy a gourmet meal served in style.

Coffee bars have sprung up like mushrooms in the last year or so. Open all day and far into the evening, they offer a wide choice of coffees, hot or cold, and a selection of appetizing snacks: finger foods such as filled baguettes, ciabatta, and easy-to-eat cakes, such as carrot cake and chocolate cake. All this is new to Norwegians but already very popular.

Most gourmet restaurants open late in the afternoon when most Norwegians still think the time has come for dinner, but tables are never full until late evening when it is dinner time for Europeans. Our habits are rapidly changing. Smaller restaurants, cafés and hotels serve breakfast, lunch and dinner. Many are open all day, so one can always get something to eat. And then, of course, there are the small street kitchens, often run by families from Eastern Europe or Asia, exciting newcomers on the Norwegian food scene who offer native specialties.

One need not be afraid of starving, and there is something to please every taste.

Norwegian produce

Strange as it may seem, our cold, wet climate has a positive effect on our produce. Pollution is still insignificant both on land and at sea, the cool growing season with its long days and short nights produces vegetables, fruits and berries that are incredibly sweet and have a rich, luscious flavor and aroma. We have healthy farm animals, pure water and a coastline that gives us seafood of exceptional quality. And anyone can walk in our woods and pick pails full of delicious wild berries – raspberries, blueberries, mountain cranberries, cloudberries, even the delicate, fruity wild strawberry that Norwegian children love to string on a straw. Woods and mountains are an Eldorado for the mushroom fancier, the hunter and the fisherman who can gather wild herbs on his way.

Fish

1n Norwegian coastal waters about 200 different kinds of fish are found. All of them are edible. In addition there are many fine fish in lakes and rivers throughout the country. In spite of this, only a very few are to be had at the fish department in the supermarket or even in specialty fish stores. When it comes to choosing fish for dinner, we Norwegians are still consistently conservative. Recently, however, we have discovered to our surprise that what we call "un-fish" are often surprisingly tasty: such delicacies as monkfish, wolf fish and the freshwater fish, pike perch, which fishermen used to throw back in the water if they got one on their hook or in their net.

Still, it is traditional fish such as cod, pollack and salmon, several types of sole, trout, herring and mackerel that are prized and eaten regularly by most of us.

Cod and salmon are special favorites. Cod is party food, while salmon, thanks to many profitable salmon farms, is food for everyday family meals.

Cod

If you ask a Norwegian, particularly from the older generations, to name his favorite dish he is very apt to say poached cod with boiled potatoes and melted butter. The secret behind a successful cod dinner is absolutely fresh fish, "live", we say. We prefer to buy our cod still swimming in a tank of salt water and let the fishmonger lift it out, gut it and clean it for us. Cod is served in finger-thick slices that are placed briefly under cold running water before they are poached in water to which 3–4 tablespoons of salt have been added for every liter. After just a few minutes the fish is lifted from the pot and placed on piping hot plates or a hot platter. The fish flesh is white and firm and flakes cleanly. Cod has a delicious nut-like flavor. Small, firm, boiled potatoes are the accepted accompaniment to poached cod, and melted butter, often with finely chopped parsley added, is poured over the fish. Red wine is traditionally served with poached cod! A meal for a lord, we say, meaning that it is good enough for the most discerning gourmet.

When the large winter cod that we call *skrei* arrives in the waters off the Lofoten islands in January, we relish a dish called *skreimølje*. The fish is served together with the roe and liver, poached in water to which vinegar, salt, whole peppercorns, bay leaves and onion are added. The creamy, flavorful liver makes butter unnecessary.

Many tons of cod are further refined to produce *tørrfisk*, and *klippfisk*.

Tørrfisk has been made in this country for over 1000 years. The cod is first cleaned, then tied together by the tail in pairs. It is then hung on racks to be thoroughly dried by the sun and wind. Thus treated, it may be stored for years in a dry place. *Tørrfisk* was an important part of the viking diet when they were on their long journeys.

Old timers like to chew the *tørrfisk* as it is, but most of us prefer it poached. Before

poaching, the fish must be soaked for 6–8 days. Most of our dried cod, however, is made into *lutefisk*, the Norwegian specialty that has become enormously popular in recent years. To make this dish the cod is first soaked, then placed in a solution of lye and water. In former times the ashes from deciduous trees were used to make the lye. In our day we use caustic soda. When the fish has soaked in the lye solution for 3–4 days it is placed in fresh water for another 2–3 days. *Lutefisk* is poached and served with boiled potatoes, bacon fat with crisply fried bits of bacon, the grease from roast pork or *pinnekjøtt*, melted butter, often with chopped hard boiled eggs added, mustard sauce or béchamel. Creamed dried peas, yellow or green, are usually served with *lutefisk*. In the north they often pour syrup and grated *geitost* (the brown Norwegian goat cheese) over the fish, and *lefse* is a must for many. *Lutefisk* is on the Christmas menu in parts of Norway.

To make **klippfisk** the cod are split down the middle, and most of the backbone is removed. The fish are then sprinkled liberally with salt and then dried. The name is derived from the time when the fish were spread on the rocks or *klipper* and dried in the open air. Now, to satisfy fastidious customers, we use modern drying methods with controlled, even temperatures. Most of the *klippfisk* that is produced in Norway is exported to countries all over the world. *Klippfisk* must be soaked in fresh water for 1–2 days before it is cooked. The best known dish made from *klippfisk* is bacalao. Fish, potatoes, onions, tomatoes and seasonings are mixed and simmered in oil to make a flavorful dish, a dish that has travelled as raw fish to Spain and back to Norway as a delicacy. *Klippfisk* may also be poached or fried and served with various accompaniments.

Another typical Norwegian dish is what we call "fish food". White fish such as haddock and wolffish are ground and made into fish balls, fish loaf or fish patties. This is everyday food that we usually buy ready made, unlike our grandmothers who made the most delicious "fish food" in their own kitchen.

Prince fish with choice accesories and a delicious sauce (recipe p. 23).

Prince fish

The story goes that this dish was first served to a Swedish prince when he was visiting Bergen some time in the 19th century. If true, it is proof that asparagus was known and appreciated in Norway a hundred years ago. As a matter of fact, it was not unusual to have asparagus growing in the garden even then.

1¼ lb (750 g) cod fillets, flayed and boned
2 tsp salt
2 small lobsters or 4–6 crayfish tails
8–12 asparagus stalks

Sauce:
2 tbsp butter
3 tbsp flour
1 cup + 3 tbsp (3 dl) veal stock
1 cup + 3 tbsp (3 dl) heavy cream
3 tbsp sherry
salt, white pepper

Cut the fish fillets into serving sized pieces. Put them in a pan, sprinkle with salt and pour over a cup of boiling water. Cover pan and let the fish stand for about 7 minutes or until it is just cooked through.

Melt the butter, stir in the flour and add stock and cream, stirring well. Simmer sauce uncovered until slightly thickened. Add sherry, salt and white pepper to taste.

Arrange the fish on a warm platter with the lobster or crayfish tails and the cooked asparagus. Pour a little of the sauce over the fish and serve the rest on the side. Pastry squares are traditionally served with Prince fish, but many prefer boiled potatoes.

Whole poached salmon

Due to our successful fish farms salmon is now available all year round. Such was not the case in the past. Then salmon was party fare that was only to be had in the summer season. It was particularly festive when the fish was poached whole.

1 salmon, approx. 3 lb
2 tsp salt
Bake for about 40 minutes in oven preset at 400° F (200° C).

The salmon we buy today is almost always gutted and cleaned. Scrub the fish well along the back bone so that all blood is removed. Remove the gills from the head, scrape the skin, rinse well and dry. Rub inside of fish with salt. Lay the fish on a large piece of aluminum foil that has been brushed with oil. Fold the foil loosely around the fish and place the package in a roasting pan with a little water in the bottom. Bake until cooked through, when the flesh is easily loosened from the back bone by a sharp knife.

Lift the whole package from the pan and turn the fish on to a warm platter. Carefully remove the skin from the side that is on top.

Serve warm with boiled potatoes and melted butter or *Sandefjord butter,* or serve it cold with horseradish sauce, boiled potatoes and cucumber salad.

Whole poached salmon may be served cold with horseradish cream and cucumber salad or warm with Sandefjord butter (recipe p. 25).

Sandefjord butter

$^3/_4$ cup (200ml) heavy cream
6 oz (200 g) unsalted butter
salt, white pepper
2–3 tbsp chopped parsley

Boil cream until reduced by half. Stir in butter a little at a time. Do not boil after the butter has been added, or the sauce will be thin. Season to taste with salt and pepper, and stir in the parsley just before serving.

Horseradish cream

1 cup + 3 tbsp (300ml) sour cream or crème fraîche
1 egg yolk (optional)
2 tsp white wine vinegar
2 tsp sugar
2–3 tbsp grated horseradish

Whip sour cream until light and fluffy. Add egg yolk if used. Season to taste with vinegar and sugar. Add horseradish.

Cucumber salad

1 cucumber
1 tbsp vinegar
$^1/_2$ tsp salt
a pinch of white pepper
1 tbsp chopped parsley

Peel cucumber if the peel is thick. Slice very thin. A vegetable peeler or a cheese plane does this neatly.

Mix vinegar, salt and pepper and pour over the cucumber. Sprinkle with parsley before serving.

The fish with accompaniments serves 6.

Pollack fillets with fried onions

Pollack is usually considered every day fare. The flesh is grayer than that of its cousin the cod. It is also firmer and has a stronger flavor. It is therefore well suited for frying.

$1^1/_4$ lb pollack fillets, boned and flayed
3 tbsp white flour or very fine whole wheat flour
1 tbsp salt
1 tsp pepper
2–3 large onions
butter or margarine for frying

Cut the fish into serving sized pieces. Mix flour, salt and pepper and dredge the fish in the mixture. Let stand until the coating sticks.

Peel the onions and slice them thin. Sauté them golden brown and tender in the butter or margarine. Keep onions warm.

Fry the fish in butter or margarine for about 3-4 minutes on each side. Fry over medium heat so the crust will be golden brown and crisp.

Serve pollack steaks with the fried onions, boiled potatoes and grated raw carrots or a green salad.

Fried trout simmered in sour cream (recipe p. 27).

Fried char with sour cream and chantarelles

We get both mountain char and the larger arctic sea char in Norway. The flesh is pink and has a strong flavor.

4 mountain char or about 2 lb arctic char
3 tbsp flour
1 tbsp salt
1 tsp pepper
3/4 cup (200 ml) water
3/4 cup (200 ml) sour cream
1 tbsp chopped parsley, chives or dill

Serve with:
2 pints cleaned chantarelle mushrooms
Clean and dry the fish. Head and tail should be left on. Mix flour, salt and pepper and dredge the fish in the mixture. Brown the fish quickly in butter or margarine. Pour off extra fat. Pour boiling water and sour cream in the pan and let the fish simmer until cooked through, 6–10 minutes depending on the size.

Clean and fry mushrooms while the fish is frying. Arrange them beside the fish on the platter.

In areas where hazelnuts grow, roasted chopped hazelnuts are often sprinkled over the fish. Boiled potatoes are served with this dish.

Variations:
Mackerel, herring, single serving sized trout, small cod and other fish may also be prepared in this way with sour cream sauce, but then the chanterelles and nuts are omitted and a salad of raw grated carrots is substituted.

Bergen fish soup

This soup is made from *pale* – young pollack. The fish is usually served separately with melted butter and potatoes but may be cut into bite sized pieces and added to the soup which is then considered the main course.

About 3 lb young pollack or other fish that make good stock, for example mackerel, flounder or perch
3 pints of water
1 cup (250 ml) milk
5 tbsp flour
2 carrots
1 parsley root
salt, pepper
approx. 1/2 cup (100 ml) thick sour cream or crème fraîche
1 tbsp chopped chives

Clean, fillet and wash the fish. Remove the gills from the head and scrub head and backbone free of blood. Put the head and bones in a roomy kettle and pour over cold water. Bring to boil and skim. Let the stock simmer uncovered for 20 minutes. If it cooks too long it will taste like glue. Strain the stock.

Bring stock to a boil. Whisk flour and milk together and add the stock, stirring constantly. Cut the fish into cubes and poach them in the stock for 5 minutes.

Clean carrots and parsley root and slice thin or dice. Cook them tender in very little water and add to the soup. Add salt and pepper to taste and stir in the sour cream just before serving. Sprinkle with chopped chives and serve piping hot. Formerly it was customary to serve pickled purslane or pumpkin in this soup.

Bergen fish soup served with pickled purslane or pumpkin (recipe p. 27). In the background, poached cod with parsley butter and boiled potatoes.

Gravlaks

Gravlaks may be bought ready to eat in all better grocery stores, either in whole fillets or smaller pieces. It is, however, easy to make your own and far tastier.

2 lb salmon fillets, the bones are removed, but the skin is left on.
2 tbsp salt
2 tbsp sugar
1 tsp coarsely ground pepper
3–4 tbsp chopped dill or other aromatic herbs such as thyme, tarragon or marjoram

Mix salt, sugar and pepper and spread some of the mixture in the bottom of a casserole or platter that is large enough for the fillets to lie flat. Sprinkle some of the herbs on the mixture. Lay one fish fillet skin side down on the platter. Spread some more of the salt mixture and the herbs on the fish, lay the other fillet on top, head to tail, with the skin up. Spread the rest of the salt and herbs on top and place a weight on the fish. Let stand at room temperature for a few hours until a brine begins to form, then place in the refrigerator or a cold cellar and let stand 3–4 days, depending on the thickness of the fillets. Turn the whole bundle once a day.

Scrape off the herbs and slice the fish very thin diagonally. Serve with mustard dill sauce (below) and bread as a first course or light supper or serve bite size for canapés.

Mustard sauce

1 tbsp mustard
1 tbsp sugar
1 tbsp white wine vinegar
$^1/_2$ tsp pepper
approx. $^1/_2$ cup (100 ml) soya oil or other oil with a neutral flavor
2–3 tbsp chopped dill

Mix mustard, sugar, vinegar and pepper. Add oil slowly, beating well as for mayonnaise until the sauce is smooth and shining. Stir in dill.

The mustard sauce may be stored in the refrigerator for as long as a week. Beat or shake well before use.

Variation: Trout, mackerel, powan and other fatty fish may be prepared and served in the same way.

Gravlaks with mustard sauce (recipe p. 29).

Meat

Fish is fish, but meat is food, said our grandparents. This goes to show that meat has always had a special place in the Norwegian diet. Meat was fancy food to be served to guests. It belonged on the table at large family gatherings and on holidays. This included both the meat from domesticated animals; lamb, pork and beef, game; such as moose, reindeer and hart, poultry; chicken, turkey and goose, and wild fowl; ptarmigan, grouse and other game birds.

For generations fresh meat was a seasonal treat that was only eaten when the farm animals were butchered in the fall or during the fall hunting season. Or perhaps an animal might be slaughtered for some very special occasion. Otherwise one had to be satisfied with dried, salted, smoked or cured meat.

In our day we can eat fresh meat all year round, and salted and cured meats are now delicacies that we bring out to vary our diet and that we are apt to serve as a special treat to guests from abroad.

Meat patties and creamed cabbage

No one can make meat patties like mother, we say, even though most mothers use precisely the same recipe! In any case, meat patties are one of our most time-honored dishes and never seem to go out of fashion.

1 lb chuck ground beef
2 tsp salt
1 1/2 tbsp potato flour or cornstarch
1/2 tsp pepper
1/2 tsp ginger
approx. 1 1/2 cup (400 ml) milk

Add salt to the ground beef and beat well until slightly stiff. Stir in potato flour or cornstarch and seasonings. Add milk a little at a time and mix well.

Shape patties and fry in butter or margarine for 4–5 minutes on each side.

Serve meat patties with boiled potatoes, creamed cabbage and wild cranberries. Many people like a good brown gravy with meat patties.

Creamed cabbage

The secret of good creamed cabbage is the nutmeg.

approx. 1 lb white cabbage
1–1 1/4 cup (200–300 ml) water
1/2 tsp salt
2 tbsp butter
3 tbsp flour
1 cup + 3 tbsp (300 ml) cabbage water
approx. 1 cup (100 ml) cream
salt, nutmeg

Dice cabbage and cook until tender in salted water. Strain off the water and set aside.

Melt butter, stir in flour and add enough cabbage water and cream to make a slightly thickened sauce. Stir well. Simmer for at least

5 minutes. Add the cabbage to the sauce and mix. Season to taste with salt and plenty of grated nutmeg.

Creamed vegetables are often served with both meat and fish. Carrots, snow peas, turnips, green beans, cauliflower, spinach and kale may all be prepared in this way.

Fresh meat and broth

In the fall when vegetables are at their best this is a popular Sunday dinner. The broth is served first with some of the vegetables. The meat is served as a separate course with the remaining vegetables, boiled potatoes and the onion sauce.

approx. 3 lb beef with the bone, shoulder, chuck or brisket
3 pints cold water
2 tsp salt
1 tsp whole peppercorns
2 bay leaves
2 parsley roots
4 carrots
1 wedge of cabbage
1 leek
1–2 tbsp chopped parsley

Ask your butcher to crack the bones in lengths suitable for the soup bowls. Put meat and bones into a large pan, pour the water over, bring to a boil and skim. Add salt, pepper and bay leaves and simmer covered for about 1 ^{1}/$_2$ hour.

Clean vegetables and place them in the pan with the meat. Simmer everything until the meat and vegetables are tender, 20–30 minutes.

Remove meat and vegetables and strain stock.

Dice some of the vegetables and return them to the soup. Sprinkle with parsley and serve the soup with flatbread on the side.

Cut the meat into neat serving pieces. Slice the rest of the vegetables and arrange them on a platter beside the meat. Serve with boiled potatoes and onion sauce.

Onion sauce

2–3 shallots, finely chopped
2 tbsp butter
3 tbsp flour
approx. 1 ^{1}/$_2$ cup (400 ml) meat stock
approx. ^{1}/$_2$ cup (100 ml) sour cream

Sauté onions in butter until soft but not brown. Sprinkle with flour, mix well and add stock, stirring smooth. Simmer for at least 5 minutes. Stir in sour cream, bring to boil and season to taste with salt.

The sauce should have a slightly tart flavor. One may substitute a little vinegar and sugar for the sour cream.

Fresh meat and broth with vegetables and onion sauce (recipe p. 33).

Mutton and cabbage

Both mutton and cabbage have always been available at all times of the year. This was therefore one of the few dishes that could be relied on for Sunday meals. Now mutton and cabbage is party food and "the friends of mutton and cabbage" gather around the pot when the season for this treat starts in the fall.

True admirers of this specialty insist on using mutton, claiming that it is more flavorful than lamb. Many, however, prefer the leaner lamb.

2 lb mutton or lamb from the shoulder or leg
2 lb cabbage
1 tbsp salt
2–3 tsp whole black peppercorns
approx. 1 pint water
Cut meat into serving sized pieces. Cut cabbage in thin wedges.

Layer meat and cabbage in a pan. Sprinkle salt and peppercorns between each layer. Add water and simmer until both meat and cabbage are tender.

Sprinkle with chopped parsley and serve with boiled potatoes. The dish is more flavorful if the peppercorns are allowed to swim freely in the pot, although many prefer to enclose them in a bit of cheesecloth or a special pepper holder.

Leg of lamb marinated in sour milk (6 servings)

Before the days of refrigerators and freezers we found other ways to keep fresh meat fresh. Marinating it was a simple solution if the meat was to be used within a week or so. Now we marinate lamb for the special flavor it gives the meat.

1 leg of lamb, approx. 4 lb
6–8 pints sour milk, such as buttermilk, kefir or unflavored yoghurt
1 tbsp salt
Roast at 320° F (160° C) for approx. 1 1/2 hours or until the meat thermometer registers 152° F (76° C).

Sauce
2 pints drippings from pan
2 tbsp flour
approx. 1/2 cup (150 ml) sour cream
salt and pepper
Place the meat in a deep dish and pour the milk over it. Refrigerate for 4–6 days. Turn meat regularly if the milk does not completely cover it. Remove meat from milk, dry and rub with salt.

Place meat on a rack in a roasting pan. Insert a meat thermometer in the thickest part. Pour a cup of water in the pan and roast until the thermometer registers 76° C. The meat should be barely done. Remove from pan and let rest about a half hour.

Deglaze the roasting pan with water and a bouillon cube. Strain. Thicken with flour mixed smooth in a little cold water. Boil sauce for at least 5 minutes, stir in sour cream and season with salt and pepper to taste.

Slice meat and serve with the sauce, potatoes and a boiled vegetable, for example green beans. Wild cranberries beaten with sugar or cranberry sauce or rowan jelly make good accompaniments.

Meat patties with creamed cabbage (recipe p. 31).

Ptarmigans with cream gravy

Formerly ptarmigan was associated with the autumn hunting season, but thanks to our freezers we can enjoy these delicious game birds all winter long.

Ptarmigan is one of the true delicacies of the Norwegian kitchen. Traditionally they are served in a cream gravy.

4 ptarmigans
4 thin slices of fat back, preferably unsalted
2 tsp salt
$^{1}/_{2}$ tsp pepper
gizzard, heart and liver
butter for browning
1 cup (250 ml) water
1 cup (250 ml) milk
$^{3}/_{4}$ cup (200 ml) sour cream or crème fraîche
1–2 tbsp currant or rowan jelly

Ptarmigans are usually sold gutted and cleaned. Dry the insides and rub with salt and pepper. Carefully loosen skin on the breast and place the fat between the skin and meat. Truss the birds and brown them evenly in the butter with the giblets.

Pour over boiling water and milk, and simmer covered over low heat for about 45 minutes or until tender dependent on the age of the birds and how long they have hung.

Remove ptarmigans from pan and cut them in two along breast and back bone. Keep warm.

Mash the liver to a paste and stir it into the stock with the sour cream or crème fraîche. Simmer gravy uncovered until it is slightly thickened, or thicken with cornstarch. Season to taste with salt, pepper and jelly.

Serve ptarmigans with the gravy, brussels sprouts or Russian peas, potatoes and rowan jelly or cranberry sauce.

Modern chefs prefer to fry only the breast meat of ptarmigan and serve them lightly cooked with the meat still pink in the middle. Brown the meat in butter in a frying pan and roast in the oven at 400° F (200° C) for 8–10 minutes. Cover bones and thighs with water and a little salt and simmer to make a rich stock. Make brown gravy using this stock and a little cream. Serve with the ptarmigan breasts.

Pork loin with crackling and sauerkraut

When we say a roast pork with a crisp rind we mean a loin of pork as it is served at Christmas throughout much of Norway. Sauerkraut and boiled potatoes are a must with this dish. Many insist on serving pork patties and sausages, too. This is heavy food that is well suited to the cold Norwegian winter.

We nearly always choose a loin that is bigger than needed for a single dinner. There should be enough to serve cold the next day. That accounts for the amounts suggested below.

4 lb pork loin with rind
2 tsp salt
1 tsp pepper
5 dl water
Roast at 360° F (180° C) for about 2 hours.
Preheat oven to 450° F (230° C).

Have your butcher score the rind into 1" squares or cut it yourself with a very sharp, pointed knife. In Norway special knives may be purchased for this purpose. Rub the pork well with salt and pepper and let it stand, refrigerated, for at least 24 hours.

Place the loin in a roasting pan with the rind down. Pour the water in the pan and

Ptarmigan with cream gravy prepared traditionally (recipe p. 37).

cover tightly with aluminum foil. Steam the meat in the oven for about 20 minutes. Remove the foil and turn the loin with rind up. Turn heat down to 180' and roast until done.

If the rind is not crisp at this point, the meat may be placed under the broiler for a minute or two.

Slice and serve warm with the pan drippings, sauerkraut and potatoes.

Sauerkraut

1 ¹/2 lb head cabbage, (white or red cabbage may be used)
2 apples
1 tsp salt
2 tsp caraway seeds
1 cup (250 ml) water or meat stock
approx. 2 tsp vinegar
approx. 2 tsp sugar

Shred cabbage with a sharp knife, pare and core apples and cut in wedges. Layer cabbage and apples in a pan with salt and caraway. Pour over water or stock and cook cabbage tender, about 45 minutes.

Season to taste with vinegar and sugar. If using red cabbage the vinegar should be added before cooking to preserve the fresh red color.

Fillet of reindeer, stag or moose

The wonderful flavor of forest and heath are best retained when the meat is served rare. Then it is also tenderest – the very best that the Norwegian kitchen can offer. The tenderloin is always tender, but many prefer a well hung sirloin because it has more flavor.

approx. 1 ¹/2 lb tenderloin or sirloin of reindeer, stag or moose
2 tsp salt
¹/2 tsp pepper
butter for browning

Sauce
³/4 cup (200 ml) meat stock
³/4 cup (200 ml) port
approx. ¹/2 cup (100 ml) heavy cream
salt, pepper

Rub the meat with salt and pepper and brown in butter in a frying pan. Place in a roasting pan and roast at 400° F (200° C) until done but still pink in the center, approx. 10–15 minutes depending on the thickness of the fillet. Let meat rest for 5–10 minutes before slicing. The slices should be about half an inch thick.

Deglaze frying pan with the stock. Add port and cream and boil until reduced by half. Season with salt and pepper to taste.

Serve the meat with the gravy, boiled small potatoes, lightly fried parsley root or other vegetables.

Roast venison with brussels sprouts and cream gravy (recipe p. 39).

Desserts

In our day most Norwegians don't eat dessert every day, usually topping off the dinner with an apple, an orange or some other fruit. But Sunday dinner and festive occasions call for dessert.

Fruit, berries, eggs, milk and cream are the most popular ingredients in Norwegian desserts. The choice usually depends on the season. In summer fresh berries; strawberries, raspberries, blueberries or cloudberries with cream are on the menu, replaced in the fall by a great variety of apple desserts. In the winter we serve puddings, hot or cold, cream mousses, dried fruit compotes or sweet thickened soups made from fruit juices.

Prune compote with vanilla sauce

For generations this has been a popular Sunday dessert. For many, however, its appearance was dreaded because it had often been boiled too long and the potato flour with which it was thickened made the sauce stringy and tough. But a light textured, well-made prune compote is not to be despised!

1/2 lb pitted prunes
1 pint (500 ml) water
3–4 tbsp sugar
1 1/2 tbsp potato flour or cornstarch

Cook prunes tender in water and sugar. Dissolve potato flour in a little cold water and stir into the prunes. Bring to a boil and take off the heat at once. Cool a little and ladle into a serving bowl.

It is also possible to use cornstarch as a thickener. The compote should then be cooked in a double boiler over hot water and stirred constantly for about ten minutes or until the raw taste of cornstarch disappears. Sprinkle a little sugar on top of the compote so a skin does not form.

Serve the compote lukewarm or serve it cold with cold vanilla sauce.

Vanilla sauce

You can buy it ready made, but it tastes better if you make it yourself.

1 vanilla bean
1 cup + 3 tbsp (300 ml) light cream
2 egg yolks
2 tbsp sugar

Split the vanilla bean lengthwise and let it steep in the cream until it reaches the boiling point.

Beat egg yolks and sugar together and beat in the hot cream. Heat the mixture to the boiling point. Cool the sauce and remove the vanilla bean. (It can be rinsed and used again). Vanilla sauce is very delicious if you stir in a little whipped cream just before serving.

Veiled farm girls

The best time to serve this delicious old time standby is in the fall when Norwegian apples are at their best.

1 cup + 3 tbsp (300 ml) applesauce
1 cup (250 ml) finely ground dried bread crumbs
3 tbsp sugar
2 tsp cinnamon
1 tbsp butter
1 cup (250 ml) heavy cream

The best applesauce is home made. Peel and core apples, cut in wedges or cubes and boil in a little water until they are soft but have not completely lost their shape. Add sugar to taste.

Mix bread crumbs with sugar and cinnamon and toast golden brown in a frying pan with the melted butter. Cool

Beat cream stiff.

Layer applesauce, crumbs and cream in a large serving bowl and top with whipped cream. Serve at once.

Can't resist

One of many delicious mousses. The name, of course, implies that it is so good that one can't resist helping oneself twice ... or more.

5 eggs
$1/2$ cup sugar
juice and grated rind of 2 lemons
1 tbsp gelatine
3 tbsp (50 ml) boiling water

Beat eggs and sugar creamy. Stir in lemon juice and grated rind.

Soften gelatine in cold water for about 5 minutes, drain and dissolve in boiling water. Cool a little and add to the egg mixture.

Stir the mousse until it begins to stiffen. Pour it in a bowl and refrigerate until set. Dip bowl in hot water for a moment, loosen the edges of the mousse with a sharp knife and turn out on a platter.

Serve with currant or raspberry sauce.

43

*Veiled farm girls
(recipe p. 43).*

Cream mold with fresh berries

This dessert may also be made with equal parts of sweet and sour cream. This gives a delicious, slightly tart flavor.

2 cups (500 ml) heavy cream
2 tbsp sugar
1 tbsp gelatine
3 tbsp boiling water
1 lb raspberries or strawberries
Soften gelatine and dissolve in hot water. Cool slightly.

Whip cream stiff with sugar and stir in gelatine.

Pour cream in a ring mold which has first been brushed very lightly with oil. Refrigerate until firm, at least 3 hours.

Turn out on a serving platter and fill the center of the mold with fresh berries.

Cloudberry cream

As early as the 1500s it was recognized, without understanding why, that cloudberries cured scurvy. Now we realize it is due to the high vitamin C content in the berries.

Cloudberries will keep for months if picked right into jars. The cover should be tightly screwed on and the jars stored in a dark, cool place. Cloudberries may also be frozen with excellent results.

2 cups (500 ml) heavy cream
$^1/_2$ lb cloudberries
sugar
Whip cream stiff and stir in the cloudberries. Sweeten to taste with sugar. Serve macaroon wreath cake or crisp cookies with cloudberry cream.

Cloudberry cream may also be made with cloudberry jam.

Other berries, such as strawberries and raspberries may be prepared in the same way. Wild raspberries are especially delicious.

Cream mold with fresh berries (recipe p. 45).

Sour cream porridge

This is not really a dessert, but can double as such if served in small portions.

Sour cream porridge has always been served on special occasions: weddings, funerals, to celebrate a birth or the harvest. Traditionally served on midsummer eve and St. Olav's day, July 29th, the recipe varies slightly in different parts of the country. Some use barley flour, others spread it over semolina pudding. Some add a little milk, others a lot. The following recipe is popular in many parts of Norway. It is not as rich as the porridge made of just sour cream.

2 cups (500 ml) sour cream
$3/4$ cup + 1 tbsp (200 ml) flour
2 cups (500 ml) milk
salt

Simmer sour cream covered for 2 minutes. Add half of the flour stirring carefully until the butter rises. Skim off the butter and keep it warm.

Stir in the rest of the flour and add milk slowly, stirring. Cook porridge 6–8 minutes. Season to taste with salt.

For a fresh, slightly tart flavor you may use half sweet and half sour milk (for example kefir).

Serve the porridge with the melted butter that was set aside, sugar and cinnamon.

For special occasions the porridge is often sprinkled with raisins or, in some parts of the country, as a gift to a new mother, with sliced hard boiled eggs.

Aquavit sorbet

Our national brandy, aquavit, always accompanies such traditional foods as cured meats, *lutefisk*, fatty foods such as pork loin and the cold buffet at Christmas, but it may also be used to flavor a delicious sorbet.

2 cups (500 ml) water
$1/2$ lb sugar
rind of 1 lemon, cut in narrow strips
juice of $1/2$ lemon
$1/2$ cup + 2 tbsp (150 ml) aquavit
1 egg white

Boil sugar, water and lemon peel for about 5 minutes. Add lemon juice. Cool and strain.

Add aquavit to taste and freeze, preferably in a sorbet machine. If you put it in the freezer, stir it often so that ice crystals do not form.

When the sorbet is half frozen, stir in the lightly beaten egg white and finish freezing.

Serve aquavit sorbet in individual serving glasses, garnish with lemon peel and lemon balm. Serve with macaroon wreath cake.

*Sour cream porridge
(recipe p. 47).*

Baking

In spite of the large selection of luscious looking cakes and other baked goods to be bought at the baker's, it is still a Norwegian tradition to bake at home. Not only at Christmas, Easter, birthdays and holidays but at other times, "on the sly", so that one always can offer a full cake tin to expected or unexpected guests.

Sweet buns

There is nothing more Norwegian than these sweet buns with their strong cardamon flavor. No children's party is complete without them, often served with hot chocolate and a dollop of cream.

For 24 buns
2 oz yeast
1 1/2 cup (350 ml) milk
4 oz butter or margarine, melted
3 oz sugar
1/2 ts salt
2 tsp cardamon
approx. 1 lb flour
egg to glaze
Bake at 450° F (225° C) for about 8 minutes.
Crumble the yeast. Heat milk to lukewarm, about 74° F (37° C), and pour over yeast. When yeast is dissolved, add melted butter, sugar, salt and flour mixed with the cardamon. Knead dough until it is smooth and elastic. Cover with plastic foil and let rise until double in bulk, about 1 hour.

Knead again lightly, roll into a long sausage and divide into 24 equal pieces. Shape into round smooth balls.

Place buns on a cooky sheet covered with baking paper and let rise about 20 minutes. Brush with lightly beaten egg and bake golden brown on the middle rack of the oven. When done the buns should have a characteristic pale ring between top and bottom.

Variations:

Raisin buns: Add approx. 1/2 cup raisins to the dough and bake as above.

Lenten buns: Cut the buns in two horizontally and fill with whipped cream. Sift powdered sugar on top. These buns are traditionally served as dessert on the first Sunday in Lent.

Hot walls: This is a Bergen specialty. Prepare dough as for sweet buns but make only 12 buns. Bake as described above. Cut a slice off the top of each bun and pour lukewarm milk flavored with cardamon over the bun, Replace top slice.

Shilling buns: Prepare dough for sweet buns. Roll dough into a rectangle, brush with lukewarm water and sprinkle with 3 tbsp sugar mixed with 2 tsp cinnamon. Roll the dough tightly from the long side, as for jelly roll, and cut into slices about 1 inch thick. Line a cooky sheet with baking paper and place slices on paper, cut side down. Let rise about 15 minutes, and bake at 400° F (200° C) for about 15 minutes.

School buns: Shape 16 buns from the above dough. Press a hollow into the middle of each bun and fill hollow with a spoonful of vanilla custard cream before buns are set to rise. Bake as above. Before serving, sprinkle with powdered sugar and coconut.

Christmas loaf: Prepare dough as above, but increase amount of butter to $^1/_2$ lb. Crumble butter into the flour mixed with $^1/_2$ lb sugar. Add 1 cup raisins and (optional) $^1/_2$ cup candied peel. Let rise. Punch down dough, divide in two and shape into round loaves. Let rise for approx. 20 minutes. Score the tops of the loaves with a sharp knife, and bake on a rack in the middle of the oven at 400° F (200° C) for about 35 minutes. Christmas loaves may also be baked in loaf pans. In that case, allow a little longer baking time.

Eat the Christmas loaf sliced, plain or buttered. The brown Norwegian goat cheese (*geitost*) is delicious with this rich bread.

Birthday wreath

In many families it is a tradition to wake the birthday child with this festive wreath of sweet yeast dough.

The wreath is set to rise in the refrigerator or other cold place. It should be eaten the day it is baked.

1 oz yeast
1 cup + 3 tbsp (300 ml) cold milk
1 egg
1 egg yolk
2 tbsp sugar
1 lb flour
$^1/_2$ lb cold butter, right from the refrigerator

Filling
$^1/_2$ lb ground almonds
1 cup powdered sugar
2 egg whites
1 egg yolk + 1 tbsp milk for glazing
coarse sugar to sprinkle on top
Bake at 450° F (225° C) for approx. 20 minutes

Mix almonds, powdered sugar and egg whites for filling.

Stir yeast in cold milk and add egg, egg yolk, sugar and flour. Roll out dough to a thick sheet. Cut cold butter into thin slices, preferably with a cheese plane, and cover $^2/_3$ of the dough. Fold dough in three, un-buttered side first. Turn dough 180° and roll out again. Fold in three. Roll to a rectangle about 8 x 30 inches. Spread the filling in a strip down the middle and fold the dough over from both sides. Cover a baking sheet with baking paper. Lay the dough, seam side down, on the paper and bend it into a large wreath. Cover well with plastic wrap and place in the refrigerator or a cool place to rise.

The next day let the wreath stand at room temperature while the oven is heating. Brush

wreath with egg yolk beaten with milk, and sprinkle with coarse sugar. Bake on bottom rack of oven until baked through and golden brown.

The wreath may also be filled with vanilla custard cream.

Princess cake

Prepare dough as for birthday wreath. Divide the dough in two, and roll out both parts. Lay one part in the bottom of a round cake pan, stretching and pressing so that it covers the bottom and sides. Spread a layer of custard cream filling over the bottom. Spread the other half of the dough with the cream filling, roll firmly as for jelly roll, and cut in thick slices. Place the slices with cut side down on the filling in the cake pan. The slices should fill the pan when risen. Let rise and bake as for the wreath.

Cream layer cake

It isn't a real party without this cake. The layers may be covered with berries and whipped cream, with vanilla custard cream, chocolate or orange cream. The top and sides may be covered with whipped cream, or with berries and flavored gelatine. The possibilities are many.

For 1 layer cake, 9 inches in diam.
3 eggs
6 tbsp sugar
$^1/_2$ cup + 3 tbsp flour
$^1/_2$ tsp baking powder
Bake at 320° F (160° C) for approx. 40 minutes
Beat eggs and sugar creamy. Mix flour and baking powder and fold into the egg mixture. Pour into a well greased spring form 9 inches in diameter. Bake on bottom rack of oven. Cool on a wire rack.

Slice the cooled cake in two horizontally.

Filling with whipped cream and berries
approx. $^1/_2$ cup apple juice or sherry
2 cups (500 ml) cream
approx. 1 cup (300 ml) good jam or fresh strawberries, raspberries or cloudberries
sugar
Moisten cake with juice or sherry. Spread a layer of jam or fresh berries on the bottom layer, sprinkle berries with sugar.

Whip cream stiff and spread half over the jam or berries. Cover with the other layer. Spread the rest of the cream on the top and sides of the cake or use a piping tube.

Marzipan cover

Follow the above recipe, but use only 1 cup cream to fill the cake. Spread a thin layer of cream over the top and sides and cover with a sheet of marzipan. This may be purchased ready to use or you can roll out your own home made marzipan (about 1/2 lb should be enough). Decorate the cake with fresh berries and fruit or with chocolate and nuts.

With custard cream filling and chocolate frosting

Moisten layers as above and spread vanilla custard cream between layers. Melt 4 oz. bittersweet chocolate and stir in 2–3 tbsp heavy cream. Cover top and sides of cake with this frosting. Decorate cake with walnut halves, marzipan hearts or sift powdered sugar over the top when the frosting has set.

Prince cake

The story goes that the recipe for this cake originally came to us with wandering craftsmen from Austria who settled in Norway. In time it became the cake we know today. It has an accepted place on the coffee table and is often baked at Christmas.

1/4 lb butter
5 tbsp sugar
2 egg yolks
2 tbsp cold water
1 tsp baking powder
1/2 lb flour

Filling
1 cup almonds
1 cup powdered sugar
2 egg whites
Bake 30–40 minutes at 380° F (190° C).
Cream butter and sugar light and creamy. Stir in egg yolks, water and flour mixed with baking powder. Cover bottom and sides of a round cake pan, about 9 inches in diam. with 2/3 of the dough. Prick bottom well with a fork.

Grind almonds and stir in powdered sugar and lightly whisked egg whites. Pour into the pan. Roll the rest of the dough into several thin ropes and place them over the cake in a grid. Brush dough with egg wash if you wish and bake on bottom rack of oven.

Prince cake will keep a long while in a tightly covered cake tin.

Macaroon wreath cake

This cake belongs to all important occasions. Decorated with flags and party snappers, it is a must at christenings, confirmations and weddings. It also appears at Christmas.

Successful macaroon should have a slightly chewy consistency that is not always easy to achieve. This cake is baked in special rings but may also be made without the molds though it is then more difficult to build an even tower.

1 lb almonds
1 lb powdered sugar
3 tbsp flour
3 egg whites
Bake about 10 minutes at 400° F (210° C).
The almonds may be unscalded, scalded or half of each. People have differing opinions about this point, but the macaroon will have a stronger flavor if at least some of the almonds are not scalded.

Grind almonds, preferably in an nut grinder and not a blender or food processor. Mix with powdered sugar and stir in slightly beaten egg whites to form an elastic dough. Press dough flat and wrap in aluminum foil. Let stand about 1 hour in oven set at 100° C.

53

The birthday child is wakened with wreath cake right from the oven (recipe p. 53), hot chocolate with cream, and gifts.

Remove and knead. Roll dough into finger thick ropes. Grease the molds very thoroughly and sprinkle well with semolina or cream of wheat. If you don't have molds shape the rings by hand. The first should be 5^1/$_2$ inches long and each successive one 1 inch longer. Bake macaroon rings in the molds or on a greased cooky sheet until golden. Cool rapidly, outdoors in the winter or in the refrigerator. Unmold and brush off excess semolina.

Pipe a glaze of powdered sugar and egg white in a scallop design on each ring, and stack the rings with the largest on the bottom to form a tall tower. Decorate the cake as you wish. In Norway we use small party snappers, flags and bonbons.

Sour cream waffles

We know of a *sæter,* a summer farm, high up among the Rondane mountains where you get sour cream waffles for breakfast! These crisp, delicious waffles, topped with jam and a dash of extra sour cream, are also a treat with your after dinner coffee.

1 cup + 3 tbsp sour cream
^{3}/$_4$ cup + 1 tbsp (200 ml) water
1^1/$_2$ cup flour
^{1}/$_2$ tsp salt
Beat all ingredients together to a smooth batter. Let swell for 15–20 minutes. Bake on a medium warm waffle iron. Lay them on a wire rack as soon as they are done so they stay crisp. Serve at once.

Beverages

Traditionally Norewegians are milk drinkers. A thirst quencher milk also was, and is, an important ingredient in food preparation. Milk was drunk at all meals where bread was served and was, of course, spread on the bread as butter or cheese. It was also soured, hung or caramelized to produce such local specialties as *dravle, mylsa, gomme,* to name just a few. Dairy products were also important because they could be exchanged for articles not produced on the farm.

Norwegians are among the world's greatest consumers of coffee, and we insist on quality coffee. Still, the coffee we drink is not always as good as it should be. We have much to learn about making coffee. The coffee bars that have sprung up in recent years have taught us that coffee is not necessarily coffee, but many different beverages, some hot, some cold.

We don't drink anywhere near as much tea as coffee, but this is changing.

Beer and mead have been drunk since the days of the Vikings. We often brewed our own beer on the farm. It was thin and sour for every day use, but strong and heady for festive occasions. Today most beer is brewed in large, commercial breweries. We produce many different types of beer with varying alcohol content. What all Norwegian beer has in common is that it is flavorful and pure. Beer is traditionally drunk as a "chaser" for our national brandy, aquavit, with many traditional Norwegian foods, as well as at Christmas and on other special occasions.

There are also many different types of aquavit. All of it is of superior quality and should therefore be drunk at room temperature.

In the fall, fruit and berries were made into jam, jelly and juice. The juice was drunk at mealtimes or as a thirst quencher. Black currant juice, rich in vitamin C, was and still is drunk warm to prevent and cure colds and sore throats. Many people enjoyed – and enjoy to this day – making wine of cultivated and wild berries, even though imported wine has also been valued in our country for generations. More recent history tells of "the upper classes" who purchased great quantities of wine in France or other wine producing countries. Wine was drunk at elegant, many course dinners in glasses that held far less than we are used to today. Hot alcohol toddies and the like were often served after dinner, though only to the "gentlemen" who

gathered around the whist table. The women had to make do with tea or now and then a glass of the housewife's homemade fruit wine or liqueur.

Mead

A popular non-alcoholic Christmas drink that both children and adults can enjoy.

8 pints water
1 lb brown sugar
1 lemon
1 bottle (300 ml) non-alcoholic sweet beer (vørter)
1 pea-sized piece of yeast
Bring water to a boil. Stir in sugar. Peel the lemon with a vegetable peeler using only the zest. Remove the white pulp from the lemon and slice fruit. Add lemon and zest to water.

Cool to 25° C. Dissolve the yeast in a spoonful of cold water and stir into the sugar water with the beer. Let the mead stand until the next day. Strain and pour into bottles. Place a sugar lump and a raisin in each bottle and cork.

Store in a cool place for a week before drinking. Mead should not be kept for more than 3–4 weeks.

Rhubarb juice

In former times everyone had a rhubarb patch in her garden, often situated behind the barn. If rhubarb first takes root it can produce huge quantities. This is a good way to make use of some of it. The juice is not very sweet and is therefore well suited to drink with meals.

3 lb rhubarb
8 pints water
$^1/_2$ lb sugar
3 tsp citric acid
Do not peel the rhubarb. Cut the stalks into 2–3 inch pieces and boil them soft in the water. Strain the juice, add sugar and stir until dissolved. Bring to a quick boil, add citric acid and skim.

Pour into warm bottles and cork at once. The juice is drunk undiluted.

Wild cranberry juice

This juice is not cooked. Even so it keeps well when it is stored in a dark, cool place. Its long shelf life is due to the fact that these berries contain natural preservatives.

2 lb wild cranberries, cleaned
2 pints water
3 tsp citric acid
$^1/_2$ lb sugar

Crush the berries and mix with the water and citric acid. Refrigerate and let stand 24 hours.

Strain juice and stir in sugar. Stir until sugar is dissolved. Skim juice and pour into bottles.

Bishop

Norway's much revered cook and cookbook writer, Hanna Winsnes, who lived in the 19th century, was a woman who enjoyed the good things of life. She also believed in doing well for "the master of the house" and the many guests who came to their home. On cold winter evenings and at Christmas it was always a pleasure to warm oneself with her "bisp" or "bishop" as she called it.

1 bottle red wine
juice of 1–2 oranges
approx. $^1/_2$ cup powdered sugar
1 piece of bitter (Seville) orange peel, coarsely crushed
boiling water

Stir orange juice and powdered sugar into the wine and add orange peel. Cover with boiling water to taste.

If you prefer a stronger taste of bitter orange you can boil the peel in a little water before mixing it in the wine.

Index of recipes

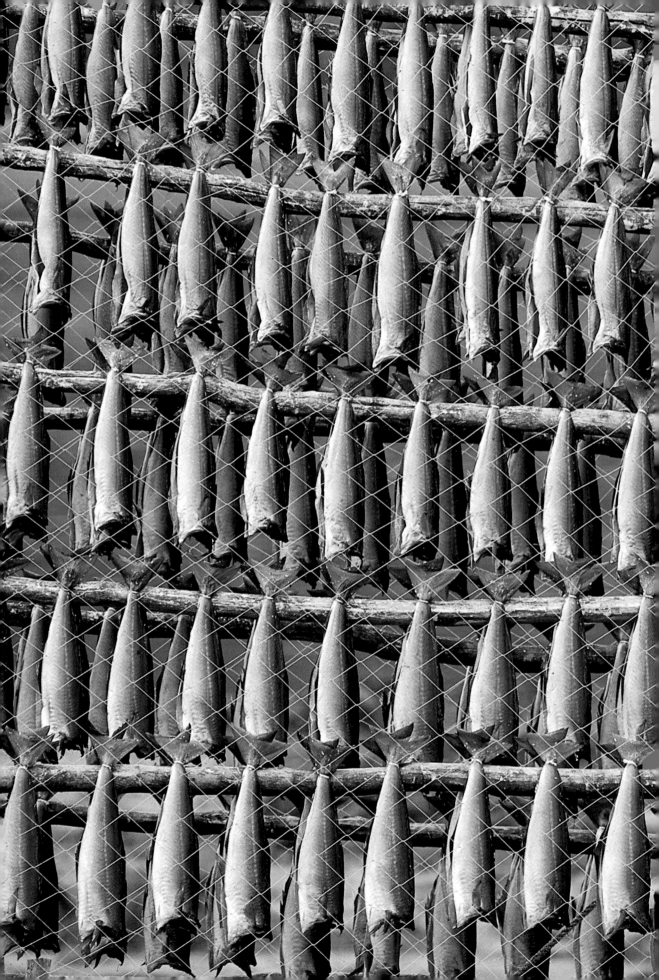